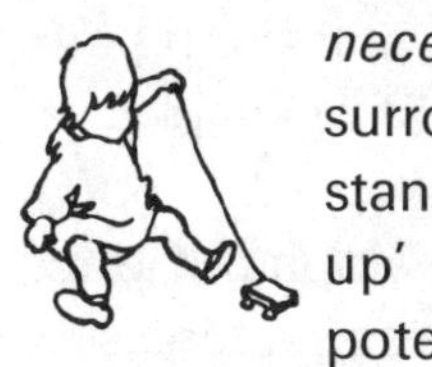

necessarily so. Res r surroundin stand up' o potent 

prise, leaving him at the age of two.

Once we realise tha umstances or our own attitudes can reduce our child's ability to develop and learn, surely we must consciously make a daily effort to help him get a little more stimulation and interest from whatever environment he is in. *At no time in his life will he develop faster than in his first two years, and we can encourage or retard his advancement.*

Maybe he has no shortage of toys, but do these toys contribute to his development? Has he handled objects big and small, soft and hard? Does he know the feel of grass, stones or leaves, tinfoil or tissue paper? Do let him find out that water will do what he wishes, that he can so masterfully fill and empty things, that sand can be pushed and pressed and stay that way, that he can use it to hide things in and discover them again. Many ordinary household articles are good play material if they are washed, loose pieces and fasteners removed, and print and paint, likely to be sucked or chewed, rubbed off with

steel wool. Cartons and boxes will stack and build like bricks, plastic bottles can be cut or shaped for water-play or as fitting toys—all giving good opportunities for helping your child's development, once you realise the significance of these materials to him. *The subsequent purchase of a really worthwhile toy is then the more easily afforded.*

When he is about one year old your baby may be ready to look at books, to hear you talk about pictures and to become familiar with words you use. Many Ladybird books are ideal for this purpose, for example: Ladybird First and Second Picture Books, The Farm, and Nursery Rhymes, etc.

At two, your child may be bursting into speech. If you have talked with him on every possible occasion whilst washing up, cooking, shopping, while in the car or at the clinic, he will have formed a sound basic vocabulary, even if he cannot yet find all the words he needs with which to express himself. His urge to communicate is there from birth, *and you are his main outlet.* Only with your co-operation in his playing and talking will he be able to develop the necessary vocabulary, the lively thinking and the understanding so essential to his mental development.

IMPORTANT NOTE TO MOTHERS: The ages given on the following pages are approximate only. All children are different and do not develop evenly. Therefore, have fun with your children and be guided by their interests.

BOOK 1
The first two years

THE LADYBIRD 'UNDER FIVE' SERIES

Learning *with* Mother

by ETHEL and HARRY WINGFIELD

Publishers: Ladybird Books Ltd . Loughborough

Printed in England

Up to seven months

We observe with delight the growth of a baby's awareness during his first few months and realise how complete a person he is. At three months he is awake for lengthening periods, and is intensely alive to the voices and movements around him.

When at about four months he can lift his head and look around, place him where you can see and talk to him while you are working, and where he can watch colour and movement, leaves fluttering, washing blowing on the line, ribbons fluttering from his pram. Indoors he can watch sunlight and shadow on moving curtains – or a colourful 'mobile' moving in a very small current of air *(see end of book)*.

At times you can carry him around the house, talking to him and letting him touch what he sees – curtains, windows, walls, furniture, carpets, taps, things smooth and rough, hard and soft, and things that glitter, rustle or tinkle. *The stimulus of contacts with objects around him will help to develop a lively mentality.*

At about seven months he will sit without support, and his drive to inspect and manipulate is intense. He transfers objects from hand to hand, tastes, feels, bangs and drops. Give scope to these new abilities by placing a variety of objects around him – household articles (made safe by washing and removing loose pieces) as well as toys.

Illustrated opposite are rings cut from a plastic container, a salt tin containing dried peas and sealed with adhesive tape, a plastic salt container (hinge removed) which will puff out air, cotton reels threaded together, and a shaving soap container holding buttons and sealed with adhesive tape.

Eight months

Try not to leave your baby alone too much. He finds the noises and movements going on around him of absorbing interest, so let him be where he can see and hear you as you work.

Your bedroom, for instance, may not be a very familiar room to him. It may contain a large mirror in which he sees the puzzling reflection of himself, as well as your reflection as you work. What fun you appear to be having with the bed clothes! He will wait in tense excitement for you to 'Boo' at him from behind the sheets. Doors and drawers open and close with clicks and bangs, clothes appear and disappear. Perhaps your dressing table contains something he could handle safely for a short while? In the kitchen there are vegetables being washed, peeled and chopped, some of which he could be given to hold and examine.

He is most interested in the washing up, in the glint of cutlery, splashing of water and clinking of crockery. If you put him where he can watch you, you will also be making a little extra time in which to talk to him, and to get the response he is now capable of giving. At this age a child has the ability to make a great variety of sounds which are his attempt to imitate your words. Without your encouragement he will not make the attempt.

Nine months

Baby's urge to learn is shown by a marked interest in detail; in the weight, shape and feel of objects. He will attempt to fit things together and take them apart again. He can grasp objects easily, but has difficulty in releasing his grasp at the right moment. Although he will happily play by himself, rolling, pushing and banging, *your company, conversation and help are important to his play.*

The toys illustrated are excellent as first fitting toys, and give practice in co-ordination of hand and eye.

Ten months

Baby is becoming increasingly capable with his hands, and can pick up very small objects with finger and thumb. He is learning about cause and effect too, and will pick up a string and pull, in order to get the toy which is fastened on the other end. He may even pull the tablecloth from the table in order to reach something he wants!

He becomes very absorbed in his play, and any extra time you can spare in which to share and encourage his activities will be well rewarded.

Eleven months

Baby will respond joyfully to finger jingles such as the familiar 'Pat-a-cake'.

He can imitate your actions and can realise that what he does amuses you also. He will want to do it again and again for the pleasure of your response.

Pat-a-cake, pat-a-cake,
Baker's man,
Bake me a cake
as fast as you can.

Prick it and pat it

and mark it with 'B'

And throw it in the oven
for Baby and me.

Eleven months

Now baby will begin to pull himself to his feet by any means available to him, and the great investigation has begun! Be sure that the fireguard is in position at all times.

You may feel that the play-pen is the safest place for him, but under your watchful eye the scope outside it can be much more stimulating. He will investigate the shopping basket, and unwrap your parcels. What excitement there is in discovering the contents! You could say, "Let's wrap it up again", "Where is it now?", "Baby find the book". Book, car, sweets, paper, are words which, together with many more, he will be attempting to repeat after you.

Do not immediately dispose of your wrapping paper; a child is as much interested in this as in the contents. Let him have it to play with, to tear a hole in, to peep through, or screw it into a ball to throw around.

Twelve months

Your baby will enjoy looking at picture books, and will be able to turn pages, but probably not one by one. Clear, simple pictures of people, animals, toys and familiar objects are ideal. He will appreciate any appropriate noises you may make and will imitate them with enthusiasm. Tell him about the pictures in simple words and short sentences, avoiding baby-talk. If he is already speaking, encourage him in his efforts to repeat your words.

Several of the Ladybird children's books are excellent for this purpose – "The Farm", the Ladybird First and Second Picture Books, etc. You can also make up a scrap book containing coloured pictures of familiar objects cut from magazines.

THE FARM
apple

Thirteen months

Here is an action rhyme he will enjoy, both for its jingling words, its boisterous action and the fact that he plays a part.

This is the way the Ladies ride
Trit-trot, trit-trot, trit-trot.

(Repeat)

This is the way
the Gentlemen ride
Gallop-a-gallop-a-gallop away.

(Repeat)

This is the way the Farmers ride
Hobble-de-dee Hobble-de-dee

(Repeat)

And down into the ditch.

Fourteen months

Baby can probably now walk unaided and his world has widened with this new achievement. He makes rapid progress in controlling his movements, and becomes involved in many new situations and discoveries – the cat next door, the cupboard under the sink, the flowers and stones in the garden, your clothes basket and even the coal hod!

Be as relaxed and permissive as is reasonably possible, using such situations for conversation and explanation. Too much negative reaction from you can dull his keenness to know and learn. At the same time it is essential to give constant attention to the danger spots in the house, flat or garden.

Fifteen months

The desire to climb is established early. The staircase provides a useful area of activity for an energetic young toddler. When your baby wants to attempt feats such as climbing stairs, getting under furniture, into cupboards or open boxes, let him do so. He is showing that the stage in his growth has been reached when he needs to attempt these things in order to advance his physical and mental development.

You can – and sometimes must – watch over his efforts for the sake of safety. Accidents at this age can evoke fear and result in the stifling of enterprise. However, a child learns caution naturally as he attempts new feats of daring.

Are you talking to him as much as possible? You can be saying: 'Up one stair – up another stair – now we are at the top. Now let's go down this way'. (Backwards, of course, and feeling for the step below).

In this sharing of play, you are helping to build his knowledge of words – 'up', 'down', 'bottom', 'top', 'stairs', 'step', 'carpet', 'wall' – all of which will become a fixed part of his vocabulary which by the age of two might well include two hundred words.

Sixteen months

Many of the containers which come into the home make splendid play material for baby. Their texture and shape will satisfy his exploring fingers. If dried peas, small pebbles, rice, etc., can be put in and the top firmly secured, the sound will add to the fun.

If you can stand the noise – and the sixteen month old certainly can – the empty tin with a wooden spoon as a drumstick makes a splendid and exciting noise. Cotton reels, plastic jars and bottles, cartons, cardboard boxes can all become play material.

The large wooden toy chest on castors is a very good toy. He can push it, ride in it, and throw his junk into it. In throwing he is learning about distance and space.

Of course, you will never let him have access to the plastic bag, glass jar or bottle, or the sharp-edged tin. Any print or paint on plastic containers can be removed with steel wool, and anything painted with lead paint *must* be avoided.

Sixteen months

Round and round the garden,
Like a teddy bear,

One step . . .

Two steps . . .

Tickle him under there.

Seventeen months

Walking is a new and major pleasure, and this type of 'fit-together' toy — which a child can build up and then pull around — will get maximum use at this age.

The 'put-together' train is made of hardwood. The base and roof of each truck are separate pieces and are joined together easily by means of fixed wooden pegs fitting into corresponding holes. The trucks link together with metal pegs which are also fixtures, ensuring that no vital pieces can be lost and the toy thereby made useless.

To actually fit together a train and then to make it move along by pulling it, gives a child a really genuine sense of achievement. To pull along this kind of toy, with the necessary looking back to see if all is well, is quite good training in balance – much more so than pushing a more rigid arrangement.

Eighteen months

Water play is the most satisfying of all play activity, taking place out of doors or, in a more restricted way, in the kitchen or bathroom. A bowl or baby bath need hold no more than safety allows. Water, warmed of course, to splash, pour or spill, to see, feel, taste and hear gives satisfaction to all his developing senses.

Plastic containers can be cut and pierced to hold water or to act as funnels and sieves. He can learn that corks, matchsticks and drinking straws will float as well as the duck from his bath, and that his bright new coin will sink to the bottom.

Nineteen months

Baby will show great interest in all the objects coming into the home. Let him examine the empty containers, cartons, boxes, wrapping paper and string. Open them flat and let him scribble on them – Chubby crayons are most suitable for this. Let him screw up or tear up paper before you dispose of it. He will love the sound, and tearing paper requires manipulative skill, as do many things he is now attempting. At no time in his life will he be learning so rapidly, and with this in mind we can supply much of the material his initiative demands at very little expense or trouble to ourselves.

If he can have the opportunity to scribble, to tear and to screw up, he will be less likely to use your wallpaper or books for this purpose. In his co-operation with you over what he is, or is not, allowed to do lies a first step in social development.

Nineteen months

Grandparents, as well as children, enjoy the traditional rhymes and jingles. Passed down from one generation to another, they enrich the vocabulary of childhood.

Leg  over  leg,

The dog .... runs to .... Dover.

(Repeat actions)

He comes .... to a .... stile

(Repeat actions)

And - UP -  he goes over.

Twenty months

To swing freely by himself, without Mother holding, is quite an adventure for a small child, creating a real sense of achievement and also increasing self confidence. There may be some small fears at first, but these are usually happily overcome, and this is yet another experience which can be enjoyed and talked about.

Try singing this jingle as your child swings :

"Swinging high and swinging low
This is the way the children go.
Down to the ground and up so high,
Just like an aeroplane in the sky."

Twenty-one months

Freedom in the garden, under an observant eye, will stimulate his developing intelligence. The smooth stones he picks up may be equal in size to his wooden building bricks, but he feels they are cold and heavy, and when he drops them into his truck they sound different – they clang and clatter. Here is your future scientist.

Please do not impose too high a standard of tidiness in his play. Too much insistence on order could at this age effectively dull his enterprise. Give him opportunity for thorough investigation of his surroundings and you will set a pattern for future concentration and sustained effort.

Twenty-two months

Baby can now use a spoon and hold a cup. Let him enjoy this skill in play with silver sand. He will fill and empty, pat and poke, pour and probably taste also (but he will soon become discouraged from doing this !). The hump and hollow in the sand are his creative effort; let him fill and talk about filling, empty and talk about emptying. Make a hole in a plastic container and let him catch the warm trickle of dry sand in his hand.

'Trickle' — that's a fascinating word to attempt !

Do not let him play with glass objects in the sand. Although he may learn care and control in doing so, the risk of serious injury is too great.

honey

Twenty-three months

Your child is now a good companion and delights to join in the work of the home and in the conversation, too. Probably he is already using a number of words, but understands many more than he can say.

A child can extend his vocabulary only by communication with adults, and only they can satisfy his need to learn. At this age, speech is closely linked with action, and your conversation with him *now* is the basis of his later education !

By encouraging your child to help you (even if 'help' is hardly the word to use !), you are setting a pattern for the years ahead when he will have developed — as a result of your patience — a real ability to see a job through from beginning to end.

Be sure to praise him for his efforts !

Two years

Make an effort to involve him in play. Play is the channel through which a child learns, and parents have wonderful opportunities particularly at this stage, to widen this learning.

The illustration opposite shows mother making imaginative use of a normal daily situation. There are countless other ways, too, in which the every-day domestic routine can expand his powers. For instance, washing up a few safe unbreakables in his own bowl and with his own mop, could give quite a lift to a child's enterprise and ability to handle articles – as well as being a lot of fun. Any activity — however insignificant it may seem — can provide an opportunity for a child to learn something worthwhile with mother.

Two years

Play material such as that shown opposite, whether purchased or improvised, develops not only physical ability but also confidence and mental stability. This age group has great difficulty in keeping still since, the head being as yet comparatively large, movement helps to keep balance.

The two year old needs to keep moving, gets great enjoyment from rough and tumble play, and attempts to do things which seem physically difficult in order to learn and acquire control and mastery of his major muscles. This type of play is of all-round importance to a growing child.

The illustration shows three boxes nailed together, a plank and a tea chest. Such material needs previous careful examination for dangerous nails, splinters or pieces of sharp metal that should be removed.

Two years

Illustrated on the opposite page are wooden nesting boxes, an abacus and a screw toy.

The nesting boxes offer a variety of play to the child. He may be well over the two years before he can balance each one correctly or nest them properly. Meanwhile, he can build with them, make the small box disappear beneath the large one and rattle one inside another. They can be pushed about in front of each other and become a train. Placed side by side they become steps, which he can demolish and build up again. He learns the meaning of big, little, up, down, inside, outside, and shows interest and preference in the colours.

The abacus has large, colourful balls which are delightful to handle. Small fingers can cup them, slide over their smooth surface and probe the large hole. In placing them onto the rods, he is learning about distance and practising his skill in releasing them at the right moment, to be rewarded by the 'plop' as they fall. Later on, the balls can be used for threading. A long tag made by stiffening one end of a length of string. with adhesive for about three inches, will make learning to thread an easier task.

A child using the screw toy needs both hands — and probably your help also — when learning to rotate his wrists in a screwing action. However, this is just one of the many skills that a child shows determination to master at about the end of its second year. The nuts can also be used for threading on a string.

Two years

If you and your child can spend snort periods together listening to rhythmic and tuneful music, music will then begin to interest the child. Instead of being mere background noise, it will be an important stimulus, encouraging the development of his sense of hearing, discrimination and rhythm. Radio, record player or simple instrument can all provide music to which to clap, dance, sway or sing, the important point being that mother and child are listening and responding together.

A Mobile

The simply constructed mobile illustrated above is also referred to on page 4. It should not be hung directly over a cot or pram in case it should fall. A very small current of air will keep it in motion.